MADAME DOUBTFIRE'S DILEMMA

FOREWORD

What impresses me so much about Dilys Rose's poetry is the extraordinary variety of her talent. Each poem is unique and complete in its metre, its metaphor and its colour. Her eye is always very intently and brilliantly fixed on the details of the natural world - its animals and fish, its birds and insects in their natural surroundings. It is a poetry which speaks with all kinds of voices - the musical voices from the pages of legend, the raucous voices from the street, the shop and the circus, the enclosing or stressful voices of the domestic scene.

As far as I'm concerned she has the power of making the heart beat rather more quickly - that's to say she is exciting and moving simply because she has looked so carefully and felt so truthfully about things, no matter whether these things are hurtful or comforting.

I think we must think of her no longer simply as a promising writer, but a writer who has spread her wings and is now soaring.

I dislike seeing mediocre writing overpraised, but I have no hesitation in writing the above, because it is a long time since I have seen one of the younger poets who has impressed me so much. To my mind she can only grow better.

Elspeth Davie

MADAME DOUBTFIRE'S DILEMMA

by

DILYS ROSE

CHAPMAN

1989

Published by
Chapman
80 Moray Street,
Blackford,
Perthshire, PH4 1QF

The publisher acknowledges the financial
assistance of the Scottish Arts Council
in the publication of this volume

British Library Cataloguing in Publication Data
Rose, Dilys 1954-
    Madame Doubtfire's dilemma. - (Chapman new writing series,
    ISSN 0953-5306)
    I. Title
    821'.914

ISBN 0 906772 23 0

Some of these poems have appeared in Cencrastus, Chapman, Glasgow
Magazine, Green Book, Fresh Oceans, Honest Ulsterman, Lines Review,
New Writing Scotland, Original Prints, The Scotsman, Writers in Brief and
have been broadcast on In Verse (STV).

*

Typeset by Lothlorien Typesetting
15 Nelson Street
Edinburgh, EH3 6LF

Printed by Mayfair Printers
Print House, William Street,
Sunderland, Tyne & Wear

CONTENTS

Cover design by Dilys Rose

NO NAME WOMAN

All day she feeds the drunken menfolk
On the terrace: between meals they gamble
Quarrel and groom their fighting cocks.
With one eye on her youngest child
(Grubbing in the dirt for bugs)
She stirs the rice, ladles broth
From spoon to bowl, fans back
The ubiquitous flies. Steaming pots
And hot fat spit their hiss at her.
She wears the same rag constantly
A hand-me-down print wrap, the pattern
Washed away, the hem a tatter -
Eats her dinner standing up
Then clears and lays more tables
Cradling plates to hush their clatter.
When only the rats nag for more
She sweeps the dirt floor clean.

TEMPLE

A jackboot-shod cop idles at the gate
Gap-tooth women ply spiced meat on sticks
The turnstile swallows tourists by the busload.

The cave's jaws brace themselves and gape,
Exhale small gasps of stale breath -
There's a smell of incense, ash and paraffin.

Way in, where a wisdom tooth might be
A spotlit Buddha glints and grins
Indifferent to flashbulb, neon - not even

A dancing flame distracts him - not even
Gifts of gold-leaf, lotus - no - he'll fast
And meditate on daylight and a breeze.

DREAM FEAST

Like pie-dogs they cower at the tail
Of every interminable queue
Alert to nothing but the sudden movement
Of a foot. They pick and scratch
At the periphery, unseeing,
Distractedly drawing
Uncertain circles in the dirt.
They're etched on the scenery.
They'll not desert for richer dunghills
But spend a lifetime praying
For windfalls, rotting morsels.
The last lean moon convinced them
They'd be mad to stray.
And so they linger, the ugly unlovable
Glut of dull-eyed waifs,
Clutching the filthy hem
Of the world's skirt.

They sleep a lot: their dreams are crammed
With sides of beef, mountains of rice.

SONG OF THE BEGGAR BOY

I see you before you see me
Mr Germany France Mr B.B.C.
Wait all day for your tourist shoes
Mr Swiss Miss U.S.
You got passports to lose
I sleep in dark doorway
Dead daddy left me
He in ditch with the crows
Crows make him bones
Look Madame Look Sir
I twist my leg round my head
Leg don't walk but it swing
Like good coco-string
Look Madame Look Sir
Hands walk if I'm fed.

PICTURESQUE

She stands - her good hand
Fanned against the noon glare.
Clad for winter all year round
In durable, customary black.
She wilts in the heat.
Her shadow dwindles, seeps
Into the bone-white walls
Which will outlive her.
She smells the air for rain,
Strains to hear the swallow-
Too much dust and a rasping drill.
Her village is pregnant with progress.
She tends her plants, now and then
Bending old eyes to fathom
A dimming horizon. Her geranium blooms
Bleed out their bright vermillion.

PHOTOREALIST

Around these parts they'll trade
A life for a bottle of beer
Here where there's only beer
Or a gun for entertainment
And the kid cadets too green
To handle either well.

Careering through the town
They scar the sky with wild fire
Round up everyone they come across
Demand documents.

The overseas reporter, swatting flies
With his clean straw hat
Heads for a rendezvous with friends
Is intercepted.

One drunk kid grabs his passport
Reads it upside down
Clears his throat to spit.
Another blows a dog to bits.

Reporter wipes away his sweat
Mimes his profession
Turns his passport right way up
Pulls out his camera as proof.

The boot boys pose, scan
Their captives, pick a victim.
And through their yells of PHOTOSCOOP
She splinters as she falls.

ORIENTAL SUNSET

Behind the backdrop of a hillside
The sky steps out of her daywear
Slips into her shot-silk evening dress.
An entourage of bats whirr and swing
At her hem, like flustered minions
Making sure she looks her best. No need.
She turns heads everywhere she goes.
As always she's immaculate. Since dawn
She's tried on every item in her wardrobe
Matching shades against the colour of her eyes.
How hard she's worked to please. And if
Her slip-shod jaded gallery is still dissatisfied

She'll dim the lights, tune up an orchestra
Of crickets, hang the moon from her sleeve.
What's more, for those who've tired of tricks
There's this: she'll entertain all night.

JOURNEY

A far throw from the glacier.
Flung on the shore of an unnamed sea
We ditched the lot, shed scales fins gills
Turned tail on the tide for an ice age.

Didn't finding our feet take our breath away?
Didn't we sway a bit, didn't our land legs
Buckle and reel at the feel of solid ground?
Didn't we long for diluted light -

A watery sun? Our dry eyes
Burned and streamed. The smell of dust
Made us thirst for the taste of salt.
We lost our tails - yes our fur fell away

But didn't we discover fire? We were bound
To tire of blunt clubs. Eventually we'd have
Hacked away at a chunk of flint. That night
Sparks flew from our hard sharp axe.

And the magic of knots - a net!
Traps set, pits dug, spits built.
And the wilderness tilled, the dam
Tapped, the wind yoked to the mill.

We slept well in those days, didn't we?
If not, we counted stars, named them
Bear, Bull, Ram - or whittled sticks
Carved charms and listened to the earth snore.

We didn't get bored, then, did we? Always
Busy with a yardstick, fencing in our scrap
Of land (extending where we could), improving
On the lock and chain, hoarding stores.

But our hourglass made us anxious
The sand ran through its bottleneck so fast.
We planned ahead with calendar and almanack
Invented tasks to outlive lifespans.

Still we felt a lack, begged augurs
Bet our fate on the flight of crows.
The alchemists worked late. In dungeons
Quacks distilled unlikely elixirs.

Slowly our taste for scrutiny refined:
Everything went under lens, lastly
Ourselves; we chopped a body down to
Fractions of less and less.

A far throw from the glacier.
Nature's close to giving up the ghost
Her secret's out, she's lost her place
To frozen embryos, the sorcery of ice.

FIGUREHEAD

The fog thickens.
I see no ships.
The gulls left days ago

Ebbing into the wake
Like friends grown tired
Of chasing failure.

I miss their uncouth snatch and grab
Their loud insatiable hunger.
I see nothing but fog.

Before my ever-open eyes
The horizon has closed in
The world's end dissolved.

I lumber on, grudging my status -
I'm purpose-built to dip and toss
My cleavage, crudely carved

To split waves
My hair caked with salt
My face flaking off.

SISTER SIRENS

Another boat veers for the perch
Where we're tethered.
We preen our feathers,
Croon seductive duets -
The sailor is deaf to all else.
He ignores omens,
Throws sense to the wind
Sets course for the harbour
Of our twin smiles.
The moon conspires with us,
Highlights our allure.
How gorgeously we glimmer.
Our glamour takes his breath away.
If only we'd squawked a warning -
    Beauty is only a trick of the light
    Beneath our flightless wings
    We've talons to tear out your heart -
If only we'd screeched,
    Block up your ears, hide your eyes
    If need be, bind yourself to the mast.

More monster than myth, we'll pick you clean.
Later we'll toss on this rocky bed,
Unable to sleep. We'll bitch, squabble
Over whose good looks charmed him ashore.

But to ourselves curse the gods
Who blessed us with the songbird's voice,
The hawk's claw.

THE LITTLE MERMAID REVISITED

She wanted so to please the master
she traded her fish tail for legs
and did not flinch when, in return,
the sea witch cut out her tongue

This girl is no mermaid though in spate
her fame came close to myth and though
each step across the master's floor
- the dusty, unheated studio,
the sloping, cruel stage,
the waxed boards of his lavish quarters -
was splintered by shards of pain,
again and again she spun for him.

No mermaid but, to enchant him,
she made her deals with the doctor,
wrenched her fractured bones
towards the lines of his aesthetic,
starved off flesh she could barely spare
implanted silicone in breasts and lips
and when the image in her mirror split
she sniffed cocaine and spun for him again.

Between bouts of derangement, despair,
she glittered on talk shows
pointed her broken toes in the air
babbled inanities on life and love,
how many hours she spent at the barre
and whether the backstage gossip was true.
Had the director led her a merry dance,
dating half of *le corps de ballet?*

The rumours were true. And though
She still held a place in his heart
And only rarely did he fail
to honour her first nights with flowers
- the flashy bouquet, the cross-kissed card
He left no address, no number.
(He'd had to cut off her strung out calls
Distress upset him. He had work to do.)

She wanted so to save the master
she traded her own skin for his,
abandoned her twitching limbs to the waves
and turned into froth.

So goes the old tale.

CARYATID

At least I'm part of a line-up
And not alone. And decently draped
In stone frills. In this condition -
Hands up forever - nakedness
Would have been unbearable.
But how my shoulders ache
Supporting the weight of your
Clever design. This elegant pose
Its inbuilt twist of the hip,
Is crippling.

What good has geometry been to me?
Couldn't I stand on two flat feet
Splayed to take the strain
Instead of aping daintiness
Faking fragility
Crushed between tons of roof and floor?
Why must I look as if I dance
Beneath my load?
I'm no footloose virgin,
Gracing an urn.

PANDORA

I'm sick of this second-hand life,
Waiting for you to come rollicking home
Drunk on glory and fit for nothing.
It's all very well, this mansion,

This patio, this expansive view
Of blue sea. My suntan is even.
The waiter brings drinks on cue.
I don't deny my luck -

It's just, for weeks I've watched figs
Darken and swell, I've wished
At the golden well and waved to boats
In the bay. Not any more. Bored,
I've taken to sleeping most of the day
Though even that has palled. All
I dream about is this same place

Its gorgeous monotony, its glut
Of luxury. Looked at too long, gilt
Dulls. And food has no taste, heat
No warmth, rest no respite. Daily,
I unlock doors, rummage in caskets,
Trunks, all except one. I'm itching
To lift the forbidden lid. Perhaps
If I did, you'd stay home more often.

QUEEN BEE

When she'd squeezed what she could
From her loyal industrious crew -

They'd plundered the sweetest blooms
Buzzed home, loudly announcing
A bumper crop, industriously
Dumping their spoils at her feet -

When she'd sweated from workers
Their last drops of toil
She summoned the housebees
To sweep out the dead.

The orgy over, her helpers
Helpless on the floor

The silence thickens around her
Like dust. She forgets herself
Ungraciously knocks back
The last of the mead.

Through gleaming corridors
Between the polyhedrons
Of her waxed and polished cell
She totters and crawls

Drunkenly weeping
Bittersweet, regal tears.

LAST CATCH OF THE NIGHT

The barrel of scallops to be shelled
Is still half-full. I pick
The prettiest first, split wide
Its tight twin fans clasped hard
Against the blade. Inside, guts
Stretch like rubber bands around
A pale marshmallow. I can't imagine
This as life: it has no parts
Which I can name, no voice for pain
No hands to mend its broken castanets
Nor legs on which to run away.
It merely shudders, and clings
To its adaptable shell.
I gouge out the edible bite
Chuck the guts overboard
Over and over. By dawn,
The big barrel's empty
The small bucket full.

AFTER THE RAIN

Look- they're underfoot
, A crop of rootless warts
Rash of pulp caps
Squatting on fat stalks
Mob of toadstools
Smug clump of puffballs
Bunched thumbstumps
Massed in ambush
(Under camouflage of leaves)
Death heads hatched in the dark

Take a boot to them
Knock their spots off.
You've had your fill?

Now look at what's upturned
The field's a spill
Of frilly broken parasols.

AS THEY FLY

Crows, in random perfection
Blow, burnt paper scraps.
The twilit sky is crowded.

Crow is anomalous:
I've ridiculed his hunchback shoulder,
Twisted toe, raucous laughter.

He has a bad name, bodes
Ill will, he's yoked
To the odour of death.

Unsociable, he plumps for
Fence-post perches
Nailed to flat fields.

He's a loner
In his crowd, aloof,
Attending to his parasites.

Like a fairground toy he's target
For an idle gun but too poor
A prize to take home.

Left as refuse, to rot.
Loudly ignored by the others,
He soon becomes compost.

Crows, flapping bedraggled feathers
Straggle to become a single brushstroke
On a darkening sky.

THE WORLD ABOUT US

They have no politics, don't mind
Which way the wind blows, they're of no
Particular persuasion - except perhaps
A bent towards another shade of green.
Adept at diplomacy, they've learnt to
Sway like limbo dancers, negotiate
For fair play from both drought and blight
And for a realistic share of day and night.

They've no religion but a heathen adulation
Of the sun. They don't indulge in bowed
Kow-towing, ignominious prostration, no not
For any superstar. Their upturned stare
Demands, their broad-leaved arms grab
All that's to be had of ultra V and infra red.
Their worship's ecumenical, it's plain -
They'll be baptised by any brand of rain.

In place of copulation there's a painless trade
With bees. It's fuss-free pollination
Involving no indignity to either gender
No debasing rut or hunt to scatter seed.
Birth occurs in silence, out of sight.
No blood is spilled. A sunk root swells
A blind shoot tunnels up through mud
A stalk bears sap to a waxing bud.

I COME HERE OFTEN

- to lie on rocks, a burning reptile,
Hear the sea's lips kiss the shore.

I come to lick salt, to infiltrate
The embrace of wave and wave.

I'm weary of my buzz-saw brain,
Wearied by the clattering of plates
And breaking hearts.

My shell has been smashed by thunder so
I feel at home with mutilated crabs
And man-made refuse.

I begrudge the gull her silent stone
Out there,

Put an ear to the ground to hear
Wet tongues on such a smooth hemline.

However,
Again,
The flood tide's drumming
Casts me adrift.

INHERITANCE

Black sack, I'll shake you off,
Burst that ballooning shadow
Insisting on the wall, rid
The night of the heavy tread
Of ominous footfalls. How I dread
Your cautionary tales. I've had
An earful of cradle nightmares
Administered like drops; bottled
Goblins, dogs with gleaming teeth
And eyes as big as saucers.
Familiars sharpen their claws
On the glass, gasping to throttle
My screams. I know them so well.

Black sack, I'll shake you off,
Banish the regions of me you inhabit,
Sleep with the light on or not at all,
Exorcise my legacy of devils.
It's lies, I say, all lies.
But when I close my eyes
They crowd the bedside
Licking their lips. I'm easy prey.

INTRODUCTION

To my ancient newborn face
Furrowed by ancestral frowns
Bloody, clenched like a fist
The world introduces itself

I'm hung upside down
Slapped by a practised hand
Air floods my lungs
Cries prove I'm alive

Brisk fingers dab and swab
The light shocks my unseeing eyes
All trace of the wet dark nest
I left behind, is dragged away.

The cord cut,
There's no going back.

BEDTIME STORY

Recently suckled. Dandled, rocked
Cuddled until my roars are quelled
My yells subside to whimpers.
I girn through lullabies
Exhaust your repertoire.
Push your patience past the limit.
Before the lids of my eyes drop shut
You'll sing yourself hoarse.
With criminal stealth I'm swaddled
Cradled by inept and weary arms
Set down. The room dimmed, you whisper,
Tiptoe. As you make a break for the door
Glance back. My face is no gypsy's ball
Gives nothing away. Goodnight.

Your sirens can scream blue murder
Bombs rip the guts from the city.
For now that's none of my business.
I won't wake until my belly's empty.
You've yet to teach me what tragedy means.
My sleep is fathoms deep.

LIKE THIS

I raise the blind
To let the sun play
On your sleeping face.
Don't wake.
It's too soon
To forsake your dreams.
For one hour more
You've all the time
In the world.
I only want to watch
Not to disturb -
You're at your best
Like this
With eyes closed
Perfectly at rest
In absolute abandon
To an inner universe.
The night's hands
Have smoothed your brow
And now daylight
Paints butterflies
on your eyelids.

INNOCENCE

They leap and spin and shout
Brash daubs of yellow red and blue
They loop-the-loop they hula-hoop
Turn somersaults and cartwheels
On the canvas of an endless day.
A simple bliss - she's not yet learnt
To mix a realistic grey and so
No clouds obscure her pure clear sky.
Only on the sun's grin a mistake -
The smudge of her purple thumb.

A DAY OUT

They pushed him into the shade
And raced for a place in the sun.
   "He's got the aviary. Adores canaries,
   Doesn't he? Besides, bright light
   Can bring on a fit."

The boy, a bulk of blankets
Slumps across his harness
See-sawing a radio from knee to knee.
Hard rock howls from an earphone
Snared in the wheelchair spokes.
No-one's near enough to see
The looping head (so way off beat)
The eyes which dart and swoop
As if to elude his view -
A monotonous box of birds gone haywire
Smashing at the mesh.

LESSON

Not your one minus one or your rule of thumb
Took me in, not abacus, calculus, logs.
I'd had it by heart but still didn't quite
Get it right so you tightened your grip
On my too small too straight chair
Till I'd learnt the square root of my fear
The sum of your anger. Total the times
I subtracted my hands from your snake-tongued stinger;
My fingers remember. That strong arm slam
(You swore it hurt you more than I) had me
Weak at the knees. I mastered deceit,
Filed wits and nails to match playground jeers.
But worse than the hot shame of tears was when
Your ruthless red pen scored up my defeat.
I can't crack your game, can't beat you yet
But I've made a start, burnt my books.

A BEGINNING

Riddled was the word the doctor used
As if he'd been devoured by woodworm.
She checked herself for being amused
By the comparison: he'd always skirt
The putting up of shelves. His skill
Was steel on steel, he tempered it
Until he snapped. "A stroke," he'd said -
His little joke - "Of fortune. Look at it
Like that." She promised him she'd try.
She did. Chalked up the years
Since half his stomach was removed -
She'd had a decade to rehearse his end.
Throw out his boots, sell off his tools?
Of course, she must get round to that
But first, she'll learn to wield
A hammer, drive a nail in straight.

MR PUNCH, THE UBIQUITOUS FARÇEUR

Ladies and Gents, I've been about.
Be in no doubt, friends, brass neck
And balls have always ensured me
A round of applause. Straight up,
I've stuck my snout in every tale
And come out winning. Here I am,
Squazzle between my teeth, a hump-back.
A pot-bellied, hook-nozzled dolt.
Cosh in one hand. Codpiece in t'other.
I've trod the boards for centuries.
Baled out Noah, consorted with Solomon.
Even in Eden, Yours Truly upstaged Adam -
    With all the vulgarity I could muster
    Filled Eve in on the nature of vice.

All that's history. Over the years
I've drawn in my belt, contented myself
With humble pie. A simple man -
Hardly the star I was. Yet in seaside
Booths of run-down resorts, there's
Still no show without Punch. But
Holding the baby was never my line.
That wife of mine has it made.
Out on the ran-dan I'll wager. Me -
My hands full of havoc. This infant
Bawls and squirms. A bald beet-red
Wriggler. Give me a dog any day.

Gave it the bottle. Didn't it sick up
Its feed? Shoved a dummy in its gob
It got spat on the floor. I swear
I tried every trick in the book.
Sang it a song, swung it sky high
(Loves it, believe me.) All useless.
The act, I grant, is a fraction hackneyed.
The bit where I knock Judy senseless
And toss the baby into the street
Has been done to death. And these days
My clean break from justice won't wash.
The public is hot for my blood. Why?
Assault and battery's all in good fun.
And always a hit with the kiddies.

MATRYUSHKA

the wooden doll widens her lidless eyes
unbinds her swaddled middle

>   *I rouge my skin, tint*
>   *alabaster lips a life-blood shade*

the doll inside unsnaps her clasp
unfolds her braided limbs

>   *I curl my hair and straighten seams*
>   *wind up my hour-glass waist*

the smaller inner wooden doll
undoes herself discards her shell

>   *I insulate my flesh in fur*
>   *perfect a veiled smile at the mirror*

inside the even smaller doll
sits the tiniest of them all

she's shapeless
faceless
plainly solid

>   *we're both indestructible now*

RAG DOLL

It doesn't feel right.
Nothing has ever been truly my own
I'm hand-me-down through and through.
It can't be me
This hotchpotch of castoffs -
What was fit for the bin
Now pads out my gut
Stuffs me until I can almost stand up.

All that I am
Is leftover, scrap
A confetti of remnants.
I'm droop-eyed, a flopsy,
My fluff head nods and lolls.
Behind my tacked-on grin
Beneath my bright gladrags
Can no-one tell I'm in shreds?
Can no-one feel me burst at the seams
For the impossible,
Long to be made new?

CHINA DOLL

Too good to cuddle in that rough-and-ready way
You play with all your toys. She's precious -
Her lace and velvet dress took mummy hours to sew,
Just like the one you wore
When you were birthday girl
The one you tore, tearing up the stairs
To rip apart the wrapper.
Look, don't touch, don't pick her up
She's best kept snug in her quilt and rug.
Her fine bone face is pale as milk
Her pretty skin is thin as eggshell -
Stop! You'll make her drop! She's delicate.
She'll not just chip, she'll break.
Her glazed blue eyes will roll away
Like mummy's dreams for you she'll shatter.
Wicked girl - don't say it doesn't matter!

DUMMY

With lace and whalebone bound
Gossamer gauze, trimmed with precision
With cords of silk pinned round
Stitched to fit the shape of the season

The tailor examines -

"When hooked up in style
You'll relish the thrill
Of the sal volatile.
Don't fret now, my dear,
Pride feels no pain.
I know that you're weak
And silly and vain
But you're pretty, my dear,
Faithful and kind.
I can take care of you,
My little hind."

With washlines and apronstrings bound
With darning and mending inbred
With blunt scissors tearing at tethers, she's found
Her breath coming thin as a thread.

MAUMET

My needs are few -
A scrap, a ragnail, any measure
Of your fear will do
So be assured -
I've no use for your face
Your place of work or pleasure
My aim never fails.
My sorcery entails no sleight of hand.
A simple plug of wax
Accommodates my every whim
My map charts out the swell
Of your soft belly
The lie of every brittle limb.
The slightest pressure of one finger
And the pin sticks firm.
Don't try to trace that ache
Back to the source
It's freelance, hiring out
Its heartlessness, to me.
Your stab at combat
Only makes things worse.
Belief in me is your curse.

FERTILITY DOLL

I'm nearly done - the belly
Like a hand-thrown bowl swells
With a homespun lack of symmetry
I swerve off-plumb.
I'm warm brown,
A baked-clay shade
Glazed to the sheen
Of egg-brushed bread.
A wholesome loaf,
Proving in the sun.

My days are numbered.
All the same my indolence
Is huge, my balance
Precarious.
This taut bulk
Threatens to topple.

The man who made me
Cut me short,
Lopped off my legs,
Stuck to the stumps
Two tiny feet.
I was a laborious task.
Now my crammed mass
Is stilted, pegged
To the earth's crust
Expecting dawn.

PERFORMING DOLL

No fairground ballerina she
With eyes like saucers
Inward spinning.
A demented doll
Taller than a tree.
Hooped round her concertina pleats
And corrugated frill
A rim of children cling.
They hold hands and their breath
And wait. The thrill begins.
From somewhere hidden in her heart
Sparks fly, the levers shunt.
And round and round she rolls
Flips up her skirt à la can-can
On each gyration. Screams
Of bright fear whirl
And spill into the night
Like catherine wheels.
The grownups on the ground
Have seen and heard it all before
And before long their gaze strays
To the automatic kick
Of monstrous lead-lined knickers.

ARTISTE

Whose high-wire have you been hired
To teeter on tonight? What trick
Will you devise to cross the netless drop
Beneath your feet? Don't look down.

Forget the ground, it's death.
For you, balance is everything.
Stay as you are - bright and far
Above the humdrum tumblers.
Stumbling clowns have always been
In on your act - as the warm-up
Applauding themselves while the gallery
Claps at their knock-down slapstick.

Don't look down. The sawdust floor
Is for blissful fools. Spangle
And flirt with the tightrope. Thrill
In being intimate with danger.

Can you hear it, the hush?
Can you feel it, the rush of fear?

You're on.

SUCCUBUS

There was no other way.
I'd tried all the usual ploys
Spruced the place up, fixed
An intimate candlelit dinner
For two. I want you to know
I went to some trouble
Took time choosing wine.
I remember when any old plonk
Would do, but let that pass.
I must say dessert was a letdown:
Not even the sensual texture of lychee
Could stir a flicker of interest.
The talk? I whisked it away
From the indigestible;
Money, the future, the bomb.
Didn't I get it right,
My role-play of bright young thing
With nothing in my head but NOW?

I never give up. No use making excuses
Clutching the bedpost, tucking up snug.
Sleep's no escape. I'm persistent
And I've got ways to have my way
With you, with or without
Co-operation. Sweet dreams.

FANTASY

In the dark she comes - piecemeal,
Touchpaper eyes to fire your desire
Open mouth a wet red pout
Collarbones and shoulderblades
Her streamlined arrows to a tilted breast
Nipple pressed against an arm
Elbow pinned to a black silk knee.

But all this can be changed,
The parts adjusted or removed
If you so wish. Each item
Holds its own particular allure.
She is designed to re-align
Her curved contours at your request.
She is, in all ways, flexible - so
Re-arrange her bend and stretch.

She's easily dismembered, stored away
Takes up no space at all.
At leisure you can re-assemble
All her interlocking pieces,
Select the size the colour
Perfume texture you require.
She's utterly reliable and
(Most conveniently)
Feels nothing.

A TRANSACTION

A word in your ear - not here, friend
The stench of despair's unbearable.
Only mass-produced wares are available
And I'll guarantee stink of ennui.

Let's thrash out the details between us -
The place is adjacent, designed
For discerning consumers like you.
No need for names at this stage.

I could tell at a glance you're particular
The cut of your suit's so precise.
As your pared fingernails graze my palm
I submit to the grip of your vice.

Discretion demands we draw down the blind
This scene could seduce the vicarious mind
I expect you're familiar with such a procedure
A man of your power. You're good for an hour.

FETISH

Whisper if you must
But the walls absorb all confession
    - I've run through this ritual so often
    If he insists, I make a confession
    Kid on his demand has me truly enthralled
    If that's not sufficient try *deeply appalled*.

Your wish, for the moment, is my command
I'm mistress of every disguise
Is it rubber fur leather or silk I've to use
To pull the wool over your eyes?
Watch me concoct your burning obsession
Spell out your lust, own up to your passion.

So that's all it was that you wanted
A secret so paltry - I'd never have guessed
It could send a man scouring the town.
A scrap of mock silk - I'm no longer impressed.
You looked like the type who'd know I don't tout
My quality goods. See yourself out.

TATTOO

He had it done last night:
Behind the blinds of Alf's Art Parlour
He scanned the well-thumbed catalogues
Until he found an apt motif.

On the left bicep TRUE LOVE presides
On the right a bloody, perforated heart
Bruised and dark as a used tea-bag.
Below, a scroll, forget-me-nots,

His girl's name etched in curlicues.
(It's near as you can get to gold
And guaranteed to come up brilliant
When the scabs have healed).

In the bar, his beer mates leer
At local girls and tease. "The lad's
Gone soft. It's tax-free booze and
Hard cash turn them on these days."

He'd wanted something durable
Hit on this hand-tooled brand
Knowing its colours would pale
Its sentiments deepen or fade.

LOCKOUT

It can't go on like this
My slamming into the night
Coatless, cashless, keyless as if
This snug city would dream
Of breaking its date with sleep.
Its doors won't give
Its entry phones act dumb
The lids of its million eyes
Are jammed shut.
The late-night dive
Has turned its sign round
To display a cardboard clock
Its hands closed on tomorrow's
Happy Hour. I rattle locks.
I'd wake the dead if I were sure
They'd take me in. At four a.m.
All that willingly opens up
Is a rain-cloud.

PERHAPS

- you're too near to see clearly.
I should have known that, closing in,
I'd lose you for a blur.
I should have known that I'd confuse
Your heart (it beats much louder
than it should) with mine.
I should have guaged the clouded lens
Set up a life-size frame of reference
Fixed your face, as if in amber,
Focussed on some gesture of repose.
I should have met you at arm's length
I should have kept my distance.

BEAUTY IS A DANGEROUS THING

- she says, hands clamped on wide hips,
Slippered feet stamping to a tune
From her youth, head thrown back,
Mirth spilling from a ragged grin.
"My dears," she says and sways
Into a song, "The things I've seen.
I'd need another life to tell you all."

ONE EYED LUIS AND THE TOURIST GIRL

That cool morning she watched him -
The cafe handyman, his bare back
To the breakfasters, his single eye
Intent on the twine he twisted
Between the chair frame and his fingers.
She took some snaps: the curve
Of his spine: his ragged shorts;
His dusty, cracked heels.

That hot afternoon he showed her
Silver fish, the breathless sea.
He spoke. She listened, heard only
The rise and fall of the language
Flowing from his throat.
The tide in his heart was turning,
The waves of his dreams breaking
On uncomprehending shores.

That humid night they danced
Cheek to cheek, eye to eye
Between locals and tourists.
He mumbled in her ear a phrase:
Te amo. That one she knew.
And she knew, as his tears
Burned her suntanned skin
How much she had to learn.

THE LOGIC OF LOVE

Though secretly he craved a harem
and orgies of multi-limbed abandon
he contented himself with a rota:
plain Jane on Mondays, rich Jane
on Wednesdays and pretty Jane all weekend.
Clever Jane he met for coffee and wit
whenever she was free. He was older
and wiser than they and nodded knowingly
- without revealing his bald spot
or his boredom - when tender loves,
with tears in their bedroom eyes,
queried his philosophy.
With practised patience, an ample supply
of hushed, hypnotic argument and
restrained but persistent fingering
of female pleasure points,
he strove to prove to each in turn
the basic flaws of jealousy.
Fidelity, he'd sigh, lowering the lights
murmuring outmoded terms of desire
as young flesh warmed to his touch,
is a dead-end for you and I.
But that was then. His students paid
lip service, learned to pass exams
in Metaphysics, Logic, Moral Phil.,
then moved on to men their own age.
He wears a wide-brimmed hat these days
to shade his eyes and cover what's left
of his hair. He sits for hours
in coffee bars, hoping that any old Jane
will stop by and, step by step,
explain where he went wrong.

CAMILLE AND MONSIEUR RODIN

If we could have lived in clay
our play, our work, our element
far from the ice bright glitter
of galleries, cafes, salons,
where the laughter at our backs
was brittle and the dull blades
of convention chiselled our love
to rubble, who knows what
might have taken shape?
Slavishly I laboured for your approval
- my knuckles permanently grazed -
and, I discovered too late
and to my cost, for the credit
of your name alone.
You told the world:
I showed her where to find gold
but the gold she finds is her own.
Monsieur, I was never your pupil,
though who wouldn't have it so?
What we both knew - and loved - flowed
back and forth between our fingers.
What didn't I do for you, who said
- when no-one was taking note -
you were nothing without me?
I gave you the gift of myself.
Model and muse, I posed to inspire
desire in all your patrons.
How many hands could refrain
from stroking my cool marble curves?
Could they imagine the fire
which formed my petrified flesh?

My mother washed her hands of me.
So did my sister. My father grieved.
My brother, for all his poetry,
did no more good than the rest
when respectability chapped at his door,
demanding that something be done
with his sister. And you, Monsieur, you
turned your gaze from my sad woman's eyes,
refused to redeem my bad woman's lies,
stopped your ears to my mad woman's cries,
let them lock up your love like a dog.

MIGRANT

How can you sit, so huge and still
Amid the vendors, beggars, the endless
Caravan of itinerants, going north, like you?
You don't even brush off the flies.
Don't the shunting trains arouse
Your curiosity? Shouldn't you
Stretch your legs, check departure times,
Watch the tail lights disappear?
Your husband will find (it's been promised)
Work; your children will be shod,
Be free of snakebite, fever, famine;
You'll drink untainted water and
Soon become used to the cold.

What brews in the cauldron of your belly?
What makes that red-slippered foot twitch?

MADAME DOUBTFIRE'S DILEMMA

Come in, come in. We're open for business
As usual. Just looking? Rummage away.
We're a bit of a muddle . . . in fact,
I'm just after telling Grace - my cat -
That a good clear out wouldn't go amiss,
Though more would be required to make
This dim damp basement shine. I confess,
My bones protest at the thought of stirring
And, truly, it goes against my grain
To shift the living. My cobwebs, I'd lose them,
My prize collection, finer than all that lace.
It clutters up the place. Reminds me of nothing
But chilled fingers, gaslight, wasted eyes.
My moths hate change. Care to view
my whirring lepidoptery, inspect the dust
Of decades dealing rag and bone?
It's there the past lies, not in a cracked vase,
A tarnished statuette. But take your time.
I won't disturb you. Wake me up if you decide
To make a purchase. Just leave me my dust.

CORNER SHOP IN A HARD WINTER

The baker's heart has gone out of his bread.
His stubborn loaves refuse to rise;
Crusts are tough, the dough flabby.
They squat on the shelf like toads.

The baker's heart has gone out of his pastries.
His cream-horn swans look shoddy, glum:
Their necks droop, wings tatter and flake.
Unsold, crumpled, weeping angelica tears.

Custom dwindles. Passers-by pass by and
Locals take their trade elsewhere,
Preferring their mouthfuls reliably bland
To the taste of baked-in despair.

DELICATESSEN

"The weather in Poland at this time of year
Is very like here, cold but bright."
His eyes drift, black olives in brine.
"The last time I was home it was spring.
The trees . . ." his hands tremble like leaves,
"Forgive me please. I talk too much."
Slicing pink discs of paprika sausage
Wrapping my 1/4 lb. in greaseproof paper
He can't help asking, "Something else?
A little cheese, perhaps some herring?"
Not today. "Okay, okay." He garnishes
His sadness with that same stale joke,
"The customer is almost always right."
The place lacks light, the warmth
Of well-stocked shelves. It reeks,
Of sour cream and slack business.
I'd go elsewhere for my sausage except
His is easily the hottest in town.

A GAEL IN GLEN STREET

No, he does not look as if
he is striding over heather
the tang of peat pricking his nostrils
sea spray lacing his cheeks with rime.
No, he does not wear tweeds
but nylon, polyester, imitation leather.
No, he does not wince in disgust
at bin bags erupting on the pavement
dusty cats licking last night's wounds
boys bouncing shouts off
a slogan-scarred church wall
a t.v. preaching to the world
about its own dark underside.
No, but he creeps along
as if on his feet
he wears ill-fitting slippers
and over his shoulders
a heavy coat of pibroch.

TOLLCROSS

He stops
half way across the street
head half turned in the direction
of oblivion
eyes half focussed on a distant miracle
or an atrocity it is hard to say
mind half way between fire
and the idea of warmth
hand half way between his pocket
and a passerby
mouth half way between a sip
and a swallow
trousers half undone
bottle half empty.
He's young.
He's been stopping
half way across the street
for years.

TARVIT STREET, 2 a.m.

From a littered stage a tireless soprano offers a final finale to flaking
cherubs. Between heaves, nonchalant propmen gossip and joke. A dust
cloud hangs in the air like a leftover special effect. Trussed for the road,
in tarpaulin, rope, the grand piano's the last load to go, nose first,
grunting and shying at the ramp, bull obstinate. The opera moves on. In
the street, local carousers shadow-waltz and serenade the neighbour-
hood with slurred, curse-laden lullabies.

EGYPTIANA IN EDINBURGH

The citizens, in freezing rain
queue to view the Pharaohs' gold
beaten by the desert poor
to shine like the merciless sun.

PHILISTINE AT THE BARBICAN

We must suppose that it took
several people
several years of study
and several further years
of climbing the architectural ladder
to be commissioned to design
from public money a fountain
which simulates
perpetual drizzle.

THE GLOBE HOTEL

Presents:
Great Entertainment
Suites for Rent
FEATURING:
Miss *NUDE* Kelowna
Leesha Ray
Marlena Skyla
PLUS
Big Boobs Week:
Miss *NUDE* Kamloops
Ashley Déjà Vu
Malibou
THE GLOBE HOTEL
Featuring
Great Suites
Entertainment for Rent
PRESENTS:
Twyla Gold
Foxy Carolla
Lipstick
PLUS
Blonde Buff Week:
Miss *NUDE* Australia
Brazil Rio
Victoria London
THE GLOBE HOTEL
Presents
Great Entertainment
Suites for Rent
FEATURING:
Candy Kiss
Loni Salomi
Tequila
PLUS
Knockout Numbers
Topaz
Twilight
Feline

COMING SOON:
Splish Splash Queens
Lysette
Minx d'Ville
Bubbles
Naughty Knotty Week
Suzy Thong
Harley
VV Venom
PLUS
Satellite Videos
Canned Music
Football (with specials)
Parking at Rear.

CHAGALL IN MONTREAL

double portrait
au verre de vin
huile sur toile

A woman in a white dress, a dark-haired, dark eyed woman, her smile something between enigma and invitation, a woman in white - perhaps her wedding dress - exposes shoulder bones, cleavage and, to the knee, one lilac-stockinged leg. One hand is white-gloved, the other (bare) fingers a fragile, oriental fan. Her slender but by no means frail shoulders support a boisterously happy man, bursting his buttons, raising aloft a celebratory glass of wine. Directly above them a baby somersaults. The stolid arches, wynds and steeples of the town are tiny, toylike. The visitors to the exhibition, touched by the laughing yellow sky, warm to each other.

TOTEM 1:

Truckstop
Towzone
Trains
Trains
Winnebago
Winnebago
Gas
Gas
Free buck
With fill up
Autobody Parts
Autobody Parlour
Autobody Shampoo
Autobody Wreckers.
Custom Hubcaps
Drive Away 2 Day
Rollalong Sportster
TravL Mate
EZ Rider
Dream on Wheels
Komfort Motor Home
Malls
Malls
Spot of Interest
Straight Ahead
Parking
Parking
Winnebago
Winnebago
Prowler
Prowler

TOTEM 2

Medicine Hat
Blackeyes Trail
Snag
Dogtooth Range
Tragedy Canyon
Heart Peaks
Bucket of Blood Saloon
Deadwood Lake
Desolation Sound
Honeymoon Bay
The Nipple
Cape Suckling
Spuzzum
Saltspring Island
Stinking Lake
Skookumchuck
Refuge Cove
Deadman's Rippled Rocks
Vermillion Forks
Hell's Gate

TOTEM 3:

hot melt glue gun
edge gel
dimetapp elixir
styling spritzer
life brand stress caplets
cashmere bathroom tissue
Puritan stews

TOTEM 4:

Loveseats:
rich in quality
beauty
and value
waterfall bag back
no sag spring seat
high skirts
padded arms
convoluted foam sandwich
posture-lock mesh
harem cushions
knife edge pleats

FOUR CANADIAN SHORTS

1. on the grave of a native child

Face down against your mother,
the enduring earth, as if to keep
the world's plague at bay
your bones clutch the dust.

2. a face in the street

Your broad flat silence is
not so much expressionless
as opaque, a bland mask,
a bandage over ancient wounds.

3. culture

Totem poles flank burger bars
in the mall and at the all-night store
on the highway a line of kids
trade beer cans for candy.

4. native art

The gallery, a reproduction longhouse
reeks of pitch, acceptability
and success. Tasteful nostalgia
is up for sale at realistic prices.

AN INTERVIEW WITH ARNGNATQUAQ

The year the caribou did not come
we arctic Ahiamuit
- The People Who Lived Apart -
starved. My husband and I outlived
that killing winter.
Our daughter did not.

Until that year the caribou
were everything to us; food,
clothing, bedding, kayaks, tents,
diapers for so many children.
We found our tribesmen frozen
at their fishing holes.

We ate bones, boiled our clothes
and chewed, spitting out hair
and our own blood. We smelled of hunger,
the smell of eating almost anything
to stay alive, and fear.
We couldn't eat our dogs.

Death did not threaten us - only
hunger's teeth tearing our guts.
We were skin and bone. So very tired.
One day my husband saw a caribou
but was too weak to chase it.
We did not eat for days.

(*Star Trek* flickers on the silent television.
Arngnatquaq brews tea.) The first white men
we saw were those who saved us,
saying that we must move no more.
This bungalow has been our home since then.
We're shackled to a fixed abode.

The old ways - bow and arrow,
trapping wolves in ice holes,
women's faces tattooed
with copper needles, black ash?
All we have left are our boots.
(Our grandchildren say they smell.)

Before we were saved we'd go to bed
hungry, cold. Now we are full
but life is not happy. Back to the igloo?
We can no longer see through blizzards.
Our teeth are too soft to chew caribou.
Now we make do with white man's food.

CROSSING THE OCEAN

What did they bring?

> Their names - to be staked on empty plots
> And later hung on house doors, streets, towns,
> Like flags pinned to a vast, uncharted map.
> Ambitions, stifled at home for generations,
> Transplanted now on tangled, stubborn scrub
> (Their sights set on taming the wilderness,
> Cultivating orchards, lawns,
> A safe place for the kids to play,
> On space space space.)
> The knack of forgetfulness
> An ache to belong
> Allegiance to endeavour
> A new-found clannishness
> Clutter of keepsakes
> Mothballed traditions
> Shards of song
> Distrust of frivolity
> Reticence deep as a mine shaft
> A tongue which turned the new world
> Round its mouth and spat it out
> Until the taste became no longer alien.

What did they leave behind?

> Their hearts, preserved
> In frame or casket
> (Given pride of place
> On a mother's mantelpiece
> Or stowed in a strongbox).
> Addresses, itineraries,
> Invitations to visit,
> Promises to keep in touch
> By aerogram and telephone.
> Friendships neglected,
> Loves doomed to stillbirth,
> Old scores unsettled.
> A future, blossoming regardless.

Dilys Rose was born in Glasgow in 1954. After a spell of teaching English in Inverness, she worked in a variety of jobs in the United States and travelled to Mexico, Greece and South East Asia. She recently spent nine months in western Canada where she took part in various writer's events including the Vancouver Writers' Festival and Harbourfront Readings, Toronto. Her first book of short stories, *Our Lady of the Pickpockets* (Secker & Warburg) was published in September 1989. She has also recently completed a collection of poems for young children. She lives in Edinburgh with her family where she visits schools under the Writers in Schools Scheme, gives readings of her work and currently reviews books for *The Scotsman*. She is working on a novel and a second collection of short stories.

CHAPMAN

Madame Doubtfire's Dilemma is the fourth of a new series of publications intended to promote new writers of outstanding talent. Many of these writers will already be known to readers of *Chapman*, Scotland's Quality Literary Magazine. This series will be chiefly devoted to poetry, but will also include prose and other writing.

If you have enjoyed reading this book, why not become a regular reader of the magazine and give it your support by subscribing. *Chapman* encourages both the writers of today and the emerging talents of the future. Sorley MacLean, Norman MacCaig, Tom Scott, Naomi Mitchison, Alasdair Gray, Jessie Kesson, Liz Lochhead, Derick Thomson, Hamish Henderson are all regular contributors.

Chapman publishes new creative writing, poetry and prose, the best in criticism and other features of cultural interest, as well as an extensive reviews section.

Subscriptions only £7.50 for 4 issues
from 80 Moray Street, Blackford, Perthshire, PH4 1QT

THE CHAPMAN NEW WRITING SERIES

RED ICE - COLIN MACKAY

". . . his is a fierce, lonely voice . . . I admire the recklessness
and the way he sustains the power and pace of the long poem
. . . the offerings are a proud display of talent." (Carol Gow,
Cencrastus)

£3.50

AVOIDING THE GODS - IAN ABBOT

"Ian Abbot has contrived for himself a disciplined mode of
utterance which can register striking correspondences with a
geography memorably observed. His uncompromising
expression of a mood and feeling seems to speak directly to
and for a spirit of place caught in natural imagery precisely
located . . . For a first book, this is an impressive debut."
(Colin Nicholson, *Lines Review)*

£3.95

BEYOND THE BORDER - JENNY ROBERTSON

"Jenny Robertson's verse has its beginnings in a deep
well of compassion; and drawn up into sun and wind,
each word falls bright and singing upon the stones of
our world . . . " (George Mackay Brown).

£3.95

SERAPION - ROBERT CALDER

A new cycle of poems in different modes of unusual range
and scope: from the moving lyric to the gripping narrative,
the biting satire to the metaphysical, establishing a
challenging, major new talent. Robert Calder is well known as
a critic, writing frequently for *Chapman* and the *Edinburgh
Review.*

£4.50